PENGUIN BOOKS
THE BEST OF LAXMAN
THE COMMON MAN STANDS IN QUEUE

Rasipuram Krishnaswamy Laxman was born and educated in Mysore. Soon after he graduated from the University of Mysore, he began cartooning for the *Free Press Journal*, a newspaper in Bombay. Six months later he joined the *Times of India* as staff cartoonist, a newspaper he has been with for over fifty years. He has written and published numerous short stories, essays and travel articles. Some of these were published in a book, *Idle Hours*. He has also written two novels, *The Hotel Riviera* and *The Messenger*, both published by Penguin Books. Penguin has also published several collections of Laxman's cartoons. *The Tunnel of Time*, Laxman's autobiography, is also available from Penguin Books.

R.K. Laxman was awarded the prestigious Padma Bhushan by the Government of India. The University of Marathwada conferred an honorary Doctor of Literature degree on him. He has won many awards for his cartoons, including Asia's top journalism award, the Ramon Magsaysay Award, in 1984.

R.K. Laxman lives in Mumbai.

R.K. Laxman

THE BEST OF LAXMAN

The Common Man Stands in Queue

PENGUIN BOOKS

Penguin Books India (P) Ltd., 11 Community Centre, Panchsheel Park,
New Delhi 110 017, India
Penguin Books Ltd., 80 Strand, London WC2R 0RL, UK
Penguin Group Inc., 375 Hudson Street, New York, NY 10014, USA
Penguin Books Australia Ltd., 250 Camberwell Road, Camberwell,
Victoria 3124, Australia
Penguin Books Canada Ltd., 10 Alcorn Avenue, Suite 300, Toronto, Ontario,
M4V 3B2, Canada
Penguin Books (NZ) Ltd., Cnr Rosedale & Airborne Roads, Albany,
Auckland, New Zealand
Penguin Books (South Africa) (Pty) Ltd., 24 Sturdee Avenue,
Rosebank 2196, South Africa

First published as *The Best of Laxman Volume III* by Penguin Books India 1994
This revised edition published 2000

Copyright © R.K. Laxman 1994, 2000

All rights reserved

10 9 8 7 6 5 4 3 2

Printed at Chaman Offset Printers, New Delhi

This book is sold subject to the condition that it shall not, by way of trade or otherwise, be lent, resold, hired out, or otherwise circulated without the publisher's prior written consent in any form of binding or cover other than that in which it is published and without a similar condition including this condition being imposed on the subsequent purchaser and without limiting the rights under copyright reserved above, no part of this publication may be reproduced, stored in or introduced into a retrieval system, or transmitted in any form or by any means (electronic, mechanical, photocopying, recording or otherwise), without the prior written permission of both the copyright owner and the above-mentioned publisher of this book.

To R.K. Narayan

INTRODUCTION

Just over a century ago the art of cartooning came to India from England and struck roots. Although other forms of art like sculpture, poetry and painting had flourished in our country for centuries, the art of graphic satire and humour was unknown. Of course both satire and humour did exist in folklore and popular poetry, poking fun at the follies of men and monarchs; the funny antics and humorous articles of the court jester were really satirical comments used to gently bring a wayward king and his band of courtiers back on track.

The role of today's cartoonist is not unlike that of the court jester of yore. His business in a democracy is to exercise his right to criticize, ridicule, find fault with and demolish the establishment and political leaders, through cartoons and caricatures.

When the British ruled, the freedom allowed to the press was limited. The role of editorial comments and cartoons was largely confined to tackling social evils like child marriage, child labour and the dowry system, or praising the efforts of the reformers. They hardly ever touched on political subjects.

Some years later the Indian cartoonist began to make timid forays into political matters. But he confined himself to attacking symbols—John Bull, for instance. When our struggle for independence from imperial domination began to gather momentum, the cartoonist gained the courage to depict real characters: the political leaders, and the viceroys and governors who were the guardians of imperial authority. Enslaved India was symbolized by an image of a suffering Indian woman called Bharat Mata—a semi-divine being adorning a crown with flowing black tresses wearing a carefully draped sari. The lady did indeed serve the purpose of inspiring patriotism in the heart of the people, inviting them to free themselves from the shackles of British imperialism.

When the British left, our leaders, who had fought for independence, settled down to draw up a respectable Constitution which would ensure freedom and equality for people who had been denied democratic liberty for centuries. India was declared a sovereign secular republic in which every citizen would enjoy liberty, equality and fraternity. The freedom of the press became particularly sacred. It was one of the most important checks to be imposed on our democratic institutions. Having drawn up such a magnificent Constitution the leaders and the led sat themselves down and looked forward to a life of peace and prosperity.

If things had worked the way our founding fathers had hoped, the cartoonist would have become an extinct species long ago. But fortunately for the cartoonist, both the rulers and the ruled unintentionally became champions of the cartoonist's cause and ceaselessly provided grist to his mill.

When Nehru took over as Prime Minister it soon became apparent to the cartoonist that he could look forward to an exciting career ahead. The aspirations of linguistic chauvinists, cow-protectors, prohibitionists, name-changers of parks and streets, all began to make their ludicrous appearance on the national scene. Our political activities became equally uproarious from he satirist's point of view. Our leaders introduced an altogether new style of functioning in our political life—hitherto unknown to the ordinary citizen. News about political parties did not concern their ideologies or their plans to help the common man, but detailed instead how intra-party groups worked against each other, squabbled amongst themselves, parted company from the party to form a new one, or defected to the very party they had opposed tooth and nail until that very moment. All this led to curiouser and curiouser political behaviour—dharnas, floor-crossing, booth-capturing, 'toppling' a chief minister, and what have you. Naturally, a cartoonist, even one with limited talent, could flourish effortlessly in this atmosphere. So, within a decade of independence, the tribe of cartoonists proliferated. New dailies, weeklies and fortnightlies published in every feasible language mushroomed everywhere, thus opening up vast opportunities for the cartoonist.

As a nation we are rather prone to talk politics—whether at a bus-stand or in a railway compartment, hobnobbing at an exclusive cocktail party or jogging in a public park. Of course, what passes for politics in these sessions is really gossip—rumour, hearsay or scandal rooted in some blurred misrepresentation of facts—concocted into a palatable mixture that is masticated between reading newspapers and magazines and listening to political news on the radio or television. That is why, though not all Indian publications are political in content, most allow for a page or two of political satire and caricature, in acknowledgement of our national pastime. Thus, the country that didn't have a single cartoonist less than a century ago is now swarming with them: good, bad and indifferent.

As I became more and more entrenched in watching and commenting on the political phantasmagoria of our country I needed an acceptable symbol to define the common Indian in my cartoons. For the cartoonist time is of the essence and the political cartoonist has the Damocles' sword of deadlines hanging permanently over his head. Many precious minutes would be lost if I were to draw elaborate masses of people composed of Maharashtrians, Bengalis, Tamilians, Punjabis and Assamese. It is easy for the cartoonist in the West where the dress and appearance of people are largely standardized, but in India there is no way of classifying an individual by the dress he wears. An industrialist, say a textile tycoon, may be dressed exactly like a retail fruit seller. Again, a scholar of Sanskrit, English, Greek and Latin might look like the humble priest of an old impoverished temple. How was I to discover and portray the common denomination in this medley of characters, dresses, appearances and habits?

In the early days I used to cram in as many figures as I could into a cartoon to represent the masses. Gradually I began to concentrate on fewer and fewer figures. These my readers came to accept as representative of the whole country. It would have been awfully anachronistic if I had attempted to prolong the presence of the Bharat Mata figure in my cartoons to symbolize the common people and their post-Independence turmoils. It would have been ridiculous, indeed, if Bharat Mata, with her crown and untied hair, holding our national flag, was seen hanging around in the background at a cabinet meeting, a glittering state banquet for a visiting foreign dignitary, or at the airport watching a worried minister dash off to Delhi. It would also not do to portray the common man in any manner one fancied, as many cartoonists did: sometimes as an old man in rags, sometimes as an emaciated individual and so on, bearing the legend 'The Common Man' on the hem of his clothes.

Eventually, I succeeded in reducing my symbol to one man: a man in a checked coat, whose bald head boasts only a wisp of white hair, and whose bristling moustache lends support to a bulbous nose, which in turn holds up an oversized pair of glasses. He has a permanent look of bewilderment on his face. He is ubiquitous. Today he is found hanging around a cabinet room where a high-powered meeting is in progress. Tomorrow he is among the slum dwellers listening to their woes, or marching along with protestors as they demand the abolition of the nuclear bomb. That, of course, does not preclude him from being present at a banquet hosted by the Prime Minister for a visiting foreign dignitary. This man has survived all sorts of domestic crises for forty years, long after the politicians who professed to protect him have disappeared. He is tough and durable. Like the mute millions of our country he has not uttered a word in all the years he has been around. He is a silent, bewildered, and often bemused spectator of events which anyway are beyond his control.

Besides my usual 'big' cartoons I started a series called *You Said It*. A single column cartoon appeared every day in the *Times of India*, in the right hand corner of the front page. The idea was to make it a free-wheeling comment on socio-economic and socio-political aspects, free of real political personalities or actual political events. The feature did not attempt any serious analysis but reflected, with a certain conscious irreverence, the general mood of the country as a whole. I expected this column to appeal to readers who were not too critical and who accepted their humdrum lot without a murmur. My taciturn Common Man, who was appearing off an on in my bigger cartoons in the company of Nehru and his cabinet ministers, came in handy for this purpose. The other characters I built around him in this single column cartoon were villagers, bureaucrats, ministers, crooked businessmen, economic experts, rebellious students, factory workers—in fact nearly every type, from every walk of life, as the occasion warranted. The column proved to be extremely popular. It has appeared every day for more than four decades, except on those all-too-brief occasions when I am on holiday!

Gathered in this volume is a selection from the thousands of cartoons I have done over the years. I am continually surprised to note that most of them are timeless in their relevance to any given moment in our history.

1 June 2000　　　　　　　　　　　　　　　*R.K. Laxman*

Simply beautiful! Where did you say the next crucial meeting of the Cabinet was to be held?

Sorry, my dear chap, this is not for bringing down the prices. This is a protest against our foreign policy!

Yes, our country is facing a lot of problems. But the difficulty is I have no time to attend to them, always having to rush from one world conference to another!

Luckily, nobody noticed it, sir! The speech you made on R-Day was the same you delivered last year!

The fund for the project is cut so drastically we could meet the cost of only the foundation-stone, sir!

Poverty, sickness, unemployment, debts, high costs, drought! What other problems? I am quite new to this ministry, you see!

OK, Pepsi isn't in the national interest. How about a chewing-gum unit with US collaboration? Are you against that too?

No, sir, I wouldn't advise you to economize. Your predecessor attempted it, resulting in a colossal wasteful expenditure!

I wish he took our walk-outs a little more seriously—everytime he jogs out like that!

... *as an eminent lawyer you ought to know that your action is tantamount to, under section B. Sub-section G.VIX, read along with I.P.C. (A) XI (B), notwithstanding* ...

The only bright news, as usual, is the PM saying that he will not tolerate violence and terrorism.

So that's a promise. You will change this new lifestyle after you get the rural votes!

The brighter side of it is that there isn't a single witness to contradict you even if you went about saying that you addressed a mammoth crowd!

This is the fourth report. It is also quite unfavourable to you! Never mind, we will order a fifth one and see.

The reputation of this office is getting from bad to worse. That chap wants to know where to give the bribe!

You had better be careful, whom you catch, constable! I shouldn't wonder if you get into trouble for this.

I demand an explanation for such confusion! What I have said there I've denied here! I want to know what exactly is the fact!

He is holding up the work, sir. He says he will not vacate till AD 2000 when he will get alternative accommodation!

He was rushed in only yesterday and now is rushing out! You can't blame the poor fellow, the conditions here are so bud!

Don't get angry with him—he wants to know what happened in the earlier parts because the poor fellow was not born when the serial started!

One moment, our talks were friendly and pleasant because you didn't discuss the dispute for which I was called!

It's nothing, sir—just gang war. I was afraid it was communal!

An anti-social element? I'm afraid you have to wait. Now he is negotiating with the militants. Later he is having a dialogue with naxalites. Then talks with terrorists . . .

You are resigning because you are disgusted with his leadership? So are we all. But aren't we sticking to him loyally? Can't you do the same?

You must retire from politics at once! Your activities are having a bad influence on him. He thinks he can get away with lying and cheating!

I still say I never met the militants! These are moderates!

You are no astrologer! You are just repeating to me all the poll analysis and speculations you have been reading in the papers!

Poor fellow is misled by rumours! He says he heard there was a bandh today and so he burnt down those buses and damaged public property!

So sorry you lost. Next time you should order a still bigger one.

That's OK, people didn't vote for you and you lost. But it's most unfair that in spite of booth capturing, rigging, intimidations, violence, he loses!

He is unlucky! Ever since he undertook it he has been called to dinner, breakfast, lunch meetings at various leaders' houses!

As an official of the IMF you will appreciate how we have reduced conspicuous consumption—Milk?

You know anything about it? He says he is new and asking which is the way to Delhi?

He is too intelligent for his age. The moment I change the channel to Doordarshan he howls!

We should have allowed only one group at a time. Now the two groups of peace marchers have clashed!

He says he is innocent and swears the assault was not pre-planned as you allege but absolutely spontaneous!

Security guard! Don't interfere with our infighting!

Hiked again, is it? That's why I stopped buying tickets a long time ago!

At last he has taken a decision! He wants to hear all the factional opinions before taking a decision!

Do you hear the noise coming from there? Get me the BBC. I want to know what's going on!

The blast damage is over here, sir!

Sure, honey, I remember the state department warning that tourists would be likely targets. But having come all the way, we've got to look around a bit!

Says you know him, sir. One Antony John, alias Abdullah, alias Siva Kumar, alias Mittu, alias Pillai, alias Chatterjee, alias . . .

Before you start, make sure whether the order is for these or those over there!

While demolishing that was the only construction which was legal!

I know, you have never been in politics. But to be on the safe side don't you think you ought to join the Congress before it's too late?

Well, he is a saviour. He provided the crucial vote to defeat the non-trust motion by defecting and joining the Congress.

What do you mean you are against the bandh? So you don't mind the multinationals coming and reducing us to beggary?

The CM and the dissident leader have collided! One was air-dashing to Delhi and the other was air-dashing from Delhi!

Pals of plants activists have won the case! We have to shift the factory from here as it is injurious to that tree!

Forget that old habit and face the camera! Remember you have been nominated and are standing for the election now!

Yet another denial? No need, sir. I am sure by now people take all your statements as denied!

Since the strike was called off we are flooded with requests to continue it, sir!

I suppose we have to take it as 'no comment'. His advisers won't let h__ say even that these days!

Only Rs 57 lakhs corruption charge against your husband? Mine is charged with over a crore!

You CBI chaps have no clue! You mean after working for over 20 years as a humble civil servant I can't afford a decent dwelling like this.

For irregularities, misconduct, misuse of office, etc., the order terminating the services has come . . . No, not to you, sir, to him!

It is sad to see these youngsters hanging around like this for admission. Remember in our days we just walked in and got our seats?

Kick-back inquiry! Next door. Scam next to that, after that pay-off, and if you go further down . . . .

When I said I wanted to survey the flood-hit areas, I thought it would be aerial survey like other ministers do.

Very kind of you to offer ... but people will say it's for health reasons if you do it, and not for our cause. So let him undertake the fast ...

Yes, it's for books, I know. But now it's for carrying cash till you get admission somewhere!

Want legal help?

They are right, sir. There is corruption in the police force. I didn't bring it to your notice because you were busy defending yourself against the pay-off allegation.

The media is unfair. I swear I told them that the remark on you was strictly off the record!

... I have threatened to self-immolate, to drown myself and I've gone on fast unto death! I will never give up. I will continue to work for our cause.

He was a freedom fighter all right. But when the Quit India call came he misunderstood it and went and became the first NRI!

No, sir, I don't understand stocks, investments, shares, receipts, loans and portfolio management. I am only a petty pick-pocket!

Clearly this is the work of anti-national elements! Pro-national elements would have only burnt buses, thrown stones, etc . . . !

Which country have you struck a deal with to smuggle in arms?

Warning to Pak, rural uplift, removal of poverty, ignorance, unemployment—remarkable. How he remembers the speech he made 27 years ago . . . !

Yes, that's me—before I decided to delink religion and enter politics!

You mean there are no dissidents in the party and no one wants to oust you? Then how do you spend your time?

You belong to the opposition, do you? Then behave in a responsible manner. I thought you were a Congress dissident.

He is here! How come he has 22 security men and you have only 18? It is insulting! You must take it up!

It's three weeks since we made sacrifices and defected to save the country and still no Cabinet post has been offered to us!

I would like to help, But what's this, 'Donations only by cheque'? What's 'cheque'?

I kept them carefully after the earlier rebellions! Return them safely for the future.

Anti-party activities have become rampant! We can't take any disciplinary action against the rebels because it would damage the party unity!

.... returning from Delhi after the lunch meet. I'll go back to catch the early flight for the breakfast meet ....

I let him go because he made sense. He said, "True, I'm a notorious gangster, extortionist, etc. But you will never find evidence to prove them!"

They will vote for me all right, if there's a mid-term poll. My work isn't finished yet—I have to give them water, food, shelter as I had promised!

If only the high command allows me to take disciplinary action against these rowdies. I will throw the whole lot out!

Excellent idea, sir, your determination to give a clean government. But it's advisable to get an OK from Delhi!

...don't know why he is so worried! He has asked me a dozen times this morning if the smugglers will be closely interrogated!

Remember the missing file which we gave up for lost, sir? We found it! It was right on your table, sir!

I am ashamed of you! How can I show my face to the public! You expect admission to any college with these miserable marks—88.75%?

No, sir, we are not reporting your statement to the press. It sounds very much like misreporting by the press!

... *we have our party intelligence sources! We know the intention of the opposition in fighting the elections! It is to defeat the Congress (I) ...*

Nonsense! Maybe he is a crook, is corrupt, has shady deals, unscrupulous, immoral etc. But you can't doubt he is a staunch nationalist!

In the ad the idea was that we all belong to one nation and that particularly, the people in my constituency, should be brought out clearly!

Good news! Remember the quick decision we took on this issue a couple of years ago? Well, there is no need to implement it. The problem has disappeared, this gentleman says.

The circular says not to let the files gather on the table. So I had a table put there and moved all of them on it.

Poor man is quite desperate this morning! He has been saying, "At a time like this what is needed is a strong government!"

What is the policy decision? Do we react like all the others saying it should have been done earlier or shall we say it should have been done later?

... *we knew we would lose here, there, our defeat came as no surprise. We lost here because of the opposition. On the whole we haven't done badly* ...

I have left strict orders—no visitors today! Not even you!

No, sir, sorry, not even their supporters—only the aspirants to the Chief Ministership are allowed in. The central observer is screening them!

You haven't ordered more powers to the police, more tightening of security, more punishment etc? Must I tell you the routine business everyday?

Do away with licensing, liberalize controls, simplify rules and encourage economic growth, you say. In short you want me to scrap my ministry!

He says he won't attend the meeting unless some senior members persuade him to come in.

My troubles are not over—I won the confidence vote!

That's all he wants—party presidentship! He has made himself one even before he has formed his new party.

Look, because we smashed their cameras and beat them up, these reporters have written all sorts of false stories about police brutalities!

I don't know what it is. If I could read I would have told you whether it is an election poster or a cinema poster!

You have procured anticipatory bail, have you? Then come down and show me the order!

I have rejected their proposal. There is nothing new in it—it is the same old offer that they will concede all our reasonable demands!

Don't announce yet! He threatens to quit if the words 'Front', 'Manch', and 'Kisan' are not included in the name of our new party!

Not to worry, sir. I am sure a mammoth crowd is watching you on the TV.

Funny, instead of the criminals they are busy chasing the policeman!

Why all this felicitation? Is it some scandal about him that Delhi has chosen to ignore?

And now some of them should quit politics and join the movies. With their years of acting experience they ought to do well!

It's an election campaign cut-out. He wants it to be propped up there whenever he is out!

No, he won't accept any engagements. He is here on a day's private visit to address two public meetings, lay a foundation stone and visit a few slums . . .

Cong (I) objects to our using that slogan! They say they have had the monopoly of it for years!

Keep off! As a loyalist I should be the first to pay tributes and call for unity in this hour of crisis!

They have drawn up the election plans—the one in the middle will be the PM. That one with a beard will be the Finance Minister. Foreign Affairs will go to...

He must have left the Congress and joined some other party—remember he came by helicopter last time?

So many modern methods are used in politics these days. I don't think there will be any hitch in arranging for a play-back speaker!

Fight for democracy, secularism etc., by all means. But it looks like you also have to fight for your deposit this time!

Sure, we will wipe out corruption, graft, immoral practices. But all these, we hope, within reasonable limits?

Are you police or army? If you are army we want help!

OK. I'll not speak if that's what you wish. But let's sit quietly for some time and then disperse!

I voted for the Congress, of course. Better to have a party in power we are used to than risk our future with some new party.

I asked them to stick all the leftover posters. That, at least, will keep the house from collapsing!

The head injury was in campaign violence, the hand in poll violence, leg in just violence!

...e waited for the ticket then. Now he is waiting for the result, later he has ... wait for Cabinet changes, portfolio allotment—poor man, he has no time ... official work.

Hey, don't say you will abolish the sales tax! The other party has offered to do that. Promise them you will get rid of the income tax, the wealth tax, etc.

Sorry, we can't give you a lift. Aren't you the chap who refused any seat adjustment with our party?

What's wrong? The idea is to use the image of a popular star to attract crowds, isn't it?

I only said, "those who have come to disturb the meeting, please leave."

You can start addressing now. For reasons of security, we couldn't let the crowd any nearer.

Seems to be a film critic He also wants you to promise that you won't go back to acting if you get defeated!

Yes, I asked all those who are against the Congress to join us—but I didn't know he had fallen out with it!

No use asking them, you silly boy! Removing poverty doesn't figure in their manifesto!

But it's factually untrue, sir! You can't say that before the officer's club gathering. We can use it in your election speech if you wish!

I lashed out at the government, yes. But how was I to know I shouldn't have? I am new to politics!

It is for showing at the election meetings how clean he is.

Garbage is not cleared in your street?—which particular garbage heap? There are so many.

I hope, sir, this move has nothing to do with my performance but only with general reorganization of the department.

How does he look? Quite decent, sir, by present standards—just wants to see you a minute to thank you personally!

Let me warn you right now. If the press reports that we quarrelled in public shamelessly it is your duty to deny it!

There are 7,50,000 people on the list waiting for new telephone connections, are there? What does it say about the rest waiting with the old connections?

A message from the Centre, sir! It says you are keeping indifferent health. You want to resign and step down before noon tomorrow, sir.

It is a malicious lie to say we topple non-Congress governments. We topple our own too like UP, Sikkim—maybe later Bihar, MP etc.

Foreign hands, sir—judging by the speeches reported in the papers.

A drinking water tap here and a school there won't do! For him to win this constituency, you have to give these people an aerodrome, a TV station, an atomic reactor complex!

At the emergency meeting everyone said you looked worried! What's the matter? I hope it has nothing to do with Punjab, J & K, Tripura, Assam, Maharashtra . . .

No bribe-tuking! No wire-pulling! No favours! No fixing things! A bunch of crooks seem to have taken over the place!

. . . and for reasons of our security and friendly ties and understanding with some countries I can't disclose something about some forces trying something to do something to our nation . . .

Our last hope is fair and free elections! We have tried out all other democratic means to topple!

Remember the 'rebel'. We were so happy that he was kidnapped? Well, he has been returned to us!

The opposition is just being nasty! There will never be a military dictatorship here! If anything it will be military democracy!

From the telephones, are you? Well, it has improved greatly, thank you. We were getting calls asking, "Modern Bun Bakery?" But now it is "State Bank of India?" or "Western Railway?"

The press and media project a false impression of our country. People everywhere are better dressed and lead a better life today than they did before.

I don't think exposed food is harmful anymore! The city has become so filthy. I am sure no fly or bacteria has survived!

All the Karnataka ministers have resigned to strengthen and keep the party! Why, if all states follow this example, it will help and strengthen the whole nation!

Your speech was good, no doubt, but the issue is so complicated, confusing and messy you blamed the CM in the end—and you happen to be the CM!

He is a cheat! I gave him Rs. 25 lakhs for defecting. Now he says he asked for that amount for his state development fund!

No new projects till our economy improves, sir? But this project is 13 years old and we have not started it yet. Shall we stop it too?

I took no bribe! I am innocent! What's more, I wouldn't touch a paltry sum of Rs 15,000 either!

Two-digit inflation doesn't bother me. I was hit by it long ago when it was just one digit.

Sorry, I can't reduce the staff. It's overstaffed, yes. But it is impossible to run my department otherwise!

Quite a few of them are around—Non-Indian Residents!

We are not afraid! We will face the situation courageously! . . . but please don't puote me!

Hold it, boys! The high command had changed its mind! We are to patch up with him! No toppling now!

It is becoming impossible to regulate the traffic with just a whistle, sir!

Very brave of you, young man, to have hit a police officer and run away.
You are under arrest, I happen to be that officer!

Election gimmick!—Looks like they are pretty nervous this time!

Yes, the subject is, "The current political crisis"—looks like he is going to trace it to its very origin!

That's the foundation-stone for the factory laid during last elections. This one is for its expansion, sir.

There's nothing we can do in South Bombay, sir! We must get the last vehicle on the Bombay–Agra Highway to back a little to ease the jam here!

Can't make out. " . . . our basic policy is to have friendly relations! But we are well prepared to face any threat . . . !" I don't know if he is talking about Pakistan or dissidents!

... *and yet he continues to say his loyalty to you is unshakeable! If we could only shake that a bit our problems could be solved!*

Superb portrayal of a wounded hero! The wounds are real, you know.

Those are loyalists. This group is dissident. These are newcomers. That's the rebel group. I don't know that solitary old man. Must be a Congressman.

How is that possible, my dear fellow? The crisis is hardly three months old and you want it to be tackled immediately!

Here is the press release; the talks collapsed as neither side could find out if the issue was economic, social, religious, political, constitutional . . .

Yes, thank you—my mission was successful. I found out there is no solution to world problems!

Ah, here it is! Today also one of the party bosses has assured that the CM won't be removed—so, that makes it full twelve days of stable government so far.

Quiet, please! No talking—copy silently or I'll send you out of the exam hall!

We shouldn't encourage big industries—that's our policy, I know. But, I say, we shouldn't encourage small industries either. If we do they are bound to become big . . . !

Of course, we are dealing with the crisis with a firm hand! We brought the situation under control—not once but six times in a single day!

Look! I haven't read this circular about cutting down on foreign jaunts—bring it to my notice after I return from my trip!

Since this meeting is just for ten minutes shall we take the world issues; arms race, Afghanistan, North-South dialogue, Lebanon, Iraq–Iran, Trade, Peace, etc. as discussed?

They still go on killing, bombing, looting, burning, threatening! We must continue to handle the situation carefully and not do anything to worsen the situation . . .

Don't you quote constitutional law! We can amend that! And don't you talk about moral law either. Now we have the right to amend that too!

Did I hear you shout for the police? Poor man, you are new around here, are you?

They say the poor chap lost heavily in the fire which burnt down his dwelling—hundreds of video cassettes, watches, Scotch bottles, foreign exchange . . . .

Don't say you will serve show-cause notice on him. As a veteran politician there is always a good cause for whatever he does!

Is it A.I.N.K.D.P. or I N.K.A.D.P. or D.K.N.I.A.P. or N.D.K.A.P.O.I. or P.O.A.I.K.D.N—this new party I formed some time ago?

He is prepared to change the party's name for the sake of opposition unity. But to ask for the change of his name also is being unfair!

Frantic search for the keys! In a non-nationalized bank this would never have happened!

Honestly, sir, we were discussing the weather!

It's my dwelling. He is my paying guest.

... OK. Have it your way, democracy was murdered! But I tell you it was a clerical error ...

Poor CM! He expanded the Cabinet so much in order to save himself. There seems to be no place for him inside!

Let go the portfolio, my dear fellow. Doing organizational work is in no way a less challenging task.

Give me a long-winded, complicated sentence to say that more land should be brought under agriculture.

He is responsible for that house collapse—he leaned against it.

These blasts were masterminded to deal a body-blow to our economy, cripple our progress and reduce us to poverty ...

I think you are finding these party problems a great strain. You always look fresh and cheerful coming home after dealing with the affairs of the nation!

*We have solved all the party problems finally and agreed to work unitedly.
I foresee no crisis hereafter for at least a week.*

It was only a minute since he was persuaded to give up the fast and he is already dashing towards the restaurant! I knew he never believed in our cause!

Stop creating panic by starting rumours! Otherwise people will attack each other, police will impose curfew, army will be called, the CM will be asked to resign ...

"I can't be a mute witness to communal disharmony, social injustice!" He said and started to paint—he is an abstract painter.

Luckily in our office there are no wooden or steel furniture!

... *and finally if the government continues to be unyielding then one of you will be asked to undertake an indefinite fast* ....

Yes. He behaved in an indisciplined manner asking you to resign! But he is not a dissident! The other one who behaved in an indisciplined manner asking you to resign is.

Here, a confidential letter to the PM. Leak it to the press first. Let me know about it.

How cleverly he is explaining with the help of those items our political, economic and social conditions to the foreign guest!

Everything is fine, so far. There have been no riots in our state. Still as a precautionary step we demand your resignation.

Nothing really wrong. The strain of the bold front he is putting in public these days is telling on him.

Yes, sir, it's a wooden thing which I carried around during the riots. It was quite handy because the order from above was not to shoot!

When he was talking of building, construction, plans and so on I thought it was some housing project. And I didn't realize it was all about mandir.

It's time to take firm action! Now I am shifting him to your place. You will be transferred to his. He will fill your vacancy and you will move over to his post . . . .

What sort of responsibility is this, catching a house-breaker instead of attending to security measures when the minister is visiting the town?

His record has been brilliant in several of his previous postings! Now, I think, he pretends to be stupid and inefficient to avoid being transferred!

. . . *you don't like me any more! Just because the studio is on strike you don't chase me round the trees singing and dancing like before!*

It may bore the listeners to hear again and again, "religion and politics should be delinked." So, make it, "politics and religion . . ." etc. etc. . . . !

At last, I've been honourably acquitted! It was a nightmare all this time! I swear I'll never again indulge in corruption!

I am told he is thoroughly demoralized after reading the poll analysis in various newspapers.

I am just thinking of my future. I'm a bachelor and can't have a dynastic rule like others. But I have a nephew . . . .

If you cut down on these wasteful expenditures he is bound to notice it and you will get into trouble. Cut down on essentials, he won't know.